How Cybercrime Targets Wealthy Families

Protect your wealth, reputation, and legacy with expert strategies to outsmart cyber threats, secure your assets, and ensure a safe, resilient future for your family in today's digital age.

Preface	3
Chapter 1 - The Modern Digital Battlefield	8
Chapter 2 - The Anatomy of Cybercrime	12
Chapter 3 - Why Wealthy Families Are High-Value Targets	16
Chapter 4 - Lessons from Real Cyber Attacks	20
Chapter 5 - Identifying Vulnerabilities	26
Chapter 6 - Protecting Non-Financial Assets	31
Chapter 7 - Inside-Out Risks,	36
Chapter 8 - The Ripple Effect!	41
Chapter 9 - Cyber Hygiene 101.	47
Chapter 10 - Cybersecurity, A Tailored Approach	51
Chapter 11 - Building Your Cyber Toolkit!	56
Chapter 12 - Creating a Culture of Cyber Awareness	61
Chapter 13 - Staying One Step Ahead!	67
Chapter 14 - Cyber Resilience.	71
Chapter 15 - Emerging Technologies in Cybersecurity.	75
Chapter 16 - The Role of Third-Party Advisors	79
Chapter 17 - Regulations and Compliance.	85
Chapter 18 - Philanthropy, ESG, and Cybersecurity	90
Chapter 19 - Cybersecurity in a Borderless World	94
Chapter 20 - The Cyber-Safe Family Office of Tomorrow	100
And Finally - Securing What Matters Most	103

Preface

Wealth attracts attention.

It always has.

But in today's digital world, that attention has moved from the obvious—fine art, luxury cars, sprawling estates—to something less tangible yet infinitely more vulnerable, your data.

For wealthy families and the family offices managing their assets, the threats have never been greater.

Cybercriminals aren't just looking for money; they're looking for access, leverage, and opportunities to exploit your trust.

This isn't fearmongering.

It's the reality of the modern world. Cybercriminals are no longer lone individuals hunched over keyboards in dark rooms.

They're organised, global, and relentless.

They use sophisticated tools and tactics to exploit vulnerabilities most people don't even know exist.

Their targets are those with the most to lose—and that includes you.

Family offices are uniquely vulnerable.

They manage not just money but also legacies, reputations, and the intricate networks of relationships that hold everything together.

A breach can do more than drain accounts; it can erode trust, destroy opportunities, and tarnish names built over generations.

The risks are personal, and the stakes couldn't be higher.

This book was born out of necessity.

For years, I've watched the cybersecurity landscape evolve.

I've seen attacks grow more sophisticated and damages climb higher.

I've seen families blindsided by breaches that could have been prevented and family offices struggling to recover from the chaos that followed.

What's clear is this, cybersecurity is no longer optional.

It's not just a technical issue; it's a business imperative.

It's a cornerstone of managing wealth in the 21st century.

The goal of this book is simple.

I want to equip you with the knowledge and tools you need to protect what matters most.

This isn't a manual filled with jargon or overly technical details.

It's a practical guide, designed to make cybersecurity understandable, actionable, and, yes, even interesting.

Because if it doesn't hold your attention, it won't hold your protection.

You'll find stories here—real ones.

Stories of wealthy families and organisations targeted by cybercriminals. Some handled the threats well; others didn't.

Each story carries lessons that apply to your world.

They show what can go wrong and, more importantly, what you can do to prevent it.

You'll also find solutions. Clear, straightforward steps you can take to build stronger defences.

From basic practices like using strong passwords and recognising phishing scams to advanced strategies involving artificial intelligence and encryption, this book covers the spectrum.

Whether you're just starting to think about cybersecurity or you already have systems in place, there's something here for you.

But let me be clear, this book isn't about selling fear.

It's about fostering confidence.

Cybersecurity doesn't have to be overwhelming.

With the right mindset and approach, it's entirely manageable.

The steps you take today can protect your family's wealth, reputation, and legacy for generations.

That's the power of being prepared.

Wealthy families face unique challenges in the digital age.

You operate in a world where privacy is elusive, and trust is fragile. Cybercriminals know this.

They exploit the very traits that make you successful—your connections, influence, and reach.

But understanding these challenges is the first step toward overcoming them.

The chapters that follow are designed to guide you through this journey.

We'll start by understanding the threat landscape—what you're up against and why you're a target.

Then, we'll move into assessing your risks, so you know where to focus your efforts.

From there, we'll explore how to build defences, create a culture of awareness, and prepare for the worst.

Finally, we'll look at the bigger picture, how cybersecurity intersects with philanthropy, ESG goals, and global operations.

By the end, you'll have a comprehensive view of what it takes to stay secure.

This book isn't just for IT experts or cybersecurity professionals.

It's for you—the executives, board members, and leaders of family offices who need to make informed decisions about protecting your assets.

You don't need to understand every technical detail to be effective.

You just need to know the right questions to ask, the risks to prioritise, and the steps to take.

Cybercrime is evolving, but so can you.

Cybercriminals rely on complacency and confusion to succeed.

By reading this book, you're taking the first step toward staying ahead. You're choosing to be proactive, informed, and prepared.

That choice matters. It's the difference between reacting to a breach and preventing one.

Between losing control and maintaining it.

Between vulnerability and resilience.

Your family's legacy deserves protection. Your reputation deserves preservation.

Your wealth deserves security.

Cybersecurity isn't just a defence—it's an investment in the future.

It's how you ensure that what you've built isn't just safe for today but enduring for tomorrow.

As you turn these pages, keep one thought in mind, the actions you take now will shape the story of your family office for years to come.

Make those actions count.

Section 1

Understanding the threat landscape

Chapter 1 - The Modern Digital Battlefield

Cybercrime has become a silent predator, lurking in the background of our digital lives, waiting for the perfect moment to strike.

For wealthy families and family offices, this isn't a distant concern—it's an immediate, growing threat.

Today's attackers are no longer petty thieves seeking a quick payday.

They are sophisticated, organised, and methodical, treating cybercrime as a business and high-net-worth families as their most lucrative targets.

In the digital age, wealth comes with an added burden, vulnerability.

Family offices, often the custodians of significant assets and personal legacies, operate in a landscape that is more exposed than ever before.

The interconnected nature of our lives—email, cloud storage, smart devices—means that every transaction, every conversation, and every click has the potential to become a weapon in the hands of a skilled hacker.

This battlefield is unlike any we've faced before.

It's not fought in boardrooms or courtrooms but in the invisible spaces of cyberspace.

And on this battlefield, wealthy families are front and centre.

Why?

Because they have everything attackers want, money, data, influence, and leverage.

The rules of engagement have changed.

Cybercriminals don't break down physical doors; they find digital ones left ajar.

A poorly secured Wi-Fi network, a reused password, or a careless click on a malicious link can serve as the gateway to a full-scale attack.

These criminals don't need guns or getaway cars—they need patience, skill, and a little luck.

And in a world where wealth management often prioritises discretion over security, luck is rarely in short supply.

Family offices are particularly vulnerable because they operate in a delicate balance between privacy and access.

They are the nerve centre of wealth management, handling everything from financial portfolios to philanthropic initiatives, often with minimal staff and fragmented systems.

This structure, designed for efficiency and confidentiality, inadvertently creates blind spots.

Cybercriminals exploit these blind spots, knowing that a breach in one area—an unsecured email account, for instance—can provide access to everything.

The implications of these breaches are staggering.

Cybercriminals don't just steal money; they steal trust.

A single attack can expose private communications, disrupt critical business deals, and tarnish reputations built over generations.

For a family office, the cost isn't just financial—it's personal.

It's the kind of damage that no insurance policy can fully cover.

On this digital battlefield, the attackers are relentless, and their methods are evolving.

They use phishing emails to trick unsuspecting employees into revealing passwords.

They deploy ransomware to hold critical systems hostage.

They leverage social engineering tactics, impersonating trusted contacts to extract sensitive information.

Their goal isn't just to infiltrate—it's to destabilise, disrupt, and profit.

For wealthy families, the stakes couldn't be higher.

The interconnected nature of their lives—spanning multiple properties, businesses, and investments—creates a vast attack surface.

Cybercriminals see these families not just as targets but as gateways.

Breaching a family office can provide access to corporate networks, influential contacts, and high-value data.

What makes this battlefield even more challenging is its invisibility.

Cyberattacks don't announce themselves with alarms or flashing lights.

They unfold quietly, often unnoticed until the damage is done.

Cybercriminals can spend months inside a system, observing, gathering data, and waiting for the perfect moment to strike.

By the time the breach is discovered, the fallout is often irreversible.

This is the new reality for family offices.

The threats are real, the attackers are sophisticated, and the consequences are severe.

But there is a silver lining, awareness is the first step toward defence.

By understanding the nature of this battlefield—its players, its tactics, and its stakes—wealthy families can begin to reclaim control.

This isn't just about installing firewalls or updating passwords.

It's about recognising that cybersecurity is as integral to wealth management as investment strategies and estate planning.

It's about shifting the narrative from reactive to proactive, from complacency to vigilance.

The modern digital battlefield is unforgiving, but it's not unbeatable. For wealthy families and family offices, survival means adaptation.

It means acknowledging that the threats are personal, the stakes are existential, and the time to act is now.

On this battlefield, there is no neutral ground.

You're either prepared or you're vulnerable.

The choice is yours.

Chapter 2 - The Anatomy of Cybercrime

Cybercrime is no longer a random nuisance.

It's a business—efficient, lucrative, and relentless.

For wealthy families and family offices, it's a business that thrives on your assets, your data, and your connections.

The digital age has brought extraordinary convenience, but it has also armed cybercriminals with tools to target, infiltrate, and exploit like never before.

To defend yourself, you must first understand the tactics they use.

Cybercriminals are not constrained by borders, time zones, or morality.

They rely on techniques that exploit human error, technical vulnerabilities, and misplaced trust.

Their attacks are not one-size-fits-all. Each strike is tailored, precise, and designed to exploit your specific weaknesses.

In the world of cybercrime, wealthy families represent the ultimate prize.

At its core, cybercrime revolves around access.

Cybercriminals want to breach your defences and gain entry to your digital life.

Once inside, they can siphon money, steal sensitive information, and dismantle trust.

Their methods are varied, but they all share a common goal, exploitation.

Phishing, for example, is one of their simplest and most effective tools.

It's designed to trick you into revealing something valuable, like a password or financial details.

The email looks legitimate—a message from your bank or a trusted advisor, urging you to act quickly.

A click on the wrong link, and suddenly the hacker is in.

They now have access to your systems, your data, and your life.

Then there's ransomware, which takes exploitation to another level.

It doesn't just steal your data; it locks you out of it entirely. Cybercriminals encrypt your files and demand payment to restore access.

For family offices, where every second of downtime can mean lost opportunities and trust, paying the ransom can seem like the only option.

But even then, there are no guarantees.

Cybercriminals may take the money and leave your systems in ruins.

Social engineering attacks prey on something even more fundamental than technology, human behaviour.

These attacks manipulate emotions—fear, urgency, trust—to make you act against your better judgment.

A hacker might pose as a lawyer, an accountant, or even a family member, creating scenarios that compel you to share sensitive information.

These aren't random stabs in the dark; they are calculated plays, backed by research into your habits, your connections, and your vulnerabilities.

Insider threats are a quieter, more insidious form of attack.

These aren't always malicious.

Sometimes, they arise from carelessness or ignorance.

A well-meaning employee reuses a password, clicks on a suspicious email, or shares access with the wrong person.

Other times, the threat is intentional—an unhappy staff member or a compromised contractor using their access to cause harm.

In either case, the damage can be catastrophic.

Cybercriminals don't operate in isolation.

They are part of an ecosystem—a global network of cybercriminals who share tools, strategies, and resources.

Some develop ransomware, others specialise in phishing campaigns, and others act as brokers, selling stolen data on the dark web.

For them, this isn't personal. It's business. And business is booming.

The frightening part is how easy it is for them to target you.

Wealthy families often have large digital footprints, spread across personal devices, family offices, and third-party vendors.

Each device, email account, or external relationship becomes a potential entry point.

Cybercriminals don't need to breach a fortress when they can walk through an open side door.

What makes cybercrime so dangerous is its stealth.

Unlike a physical break-in, you won't know it's happening until it's too late.

Cybercriminals can spend weeks or months inside your systems, watching, gathering information, and waiting for the right moment to strike.

They don't just want to break in—they want to stay in, using your systems as a base to launch further attacks or siphon more data over time.

The anatomy of cybercrime is built on patience, precision, and persistence.

Cybercriminals are not in a hurry.

They know the value of what they're targeting, and they're willing to invest time and effort to get it.

They don't need to hit every target—just a few successful breaches can yield massive returns.

For family offices, the stakes couldn't be higher.

These attacks aren't just about financial loss.

They're about control.

A breach can expose personal details, disrupt operations, and erode trust.

The aftermath often lingers long after the immediate threat is resolved, as families grapple with reputational damage and lingering vulnerabilities.

Understanding the anatomy of cybercrime isn't just academic.

It's essential for survival. When you know how cybercriminals operate—how they infiltrate, exploit, and escape—you can begin to identify the weak points in your own defences.

This knowledge doesn't just empower you; it makes you a harder target.

Cybercrime thrives on one thing, unpreparedness.

The good news is that preparation is within your control.

But it starts here, with understanding.

In this modern digital battlefield, knowing your enemy is the first step to winning the fight.

Chapter 3 - Why Wealthy Families Are High-Value Targets

Wealthy families and family offices live in a paradox.

The very privacy they guard so fiercely can often make them easier targets for cybercriminals.

Cybercriminals see these families as treasure troves of opportunity—valuable assets, sensitive data, and reputations that can be leveraged for ransom or destruction.

Unlike large corporations with well-funded cybersecurity departments, family offices frequently operate in relative obscurity, assuming their lower profile provides a natural shield.

But in the digital world, that assumption couldn't be more dangerous.

Cybercriminals are drawn to wealthy families not just because of the zeros in their bank accounts but because of what wealth represents, influence, access, and connections.

These criminals aren't haphazard opportunists.

They are methodical, treating cybercrime like a business venture.

They research their targets, learning about their personal lives, professional networks, and even philanthropic interests.

What's alarming is how little effort it takes to find this information.

A single news article, a charity gala mention, or a vacation photo on social media can provide all the clues a hacker needs to launch an attack.

For cybercriminals, family offices represent a unique combination of complexity and vulnerability.

The sprawling networks of advisors, vendors, and staff create a web of potential entry points.

A poorly secured email account or a shared Wi-Fi network at a holiday home can serve as an open door.

The digital landscape amplifies these risks, making it easier than ever for attackers to infiltrate, observe, and wait for the perfect moment to strike.

The allure of wealthy families extends beyond money.

Cybercriminals are acutely aware of the reputational stakes involved.

They know that for a family with significant public visibility or influence, a leaked email chain or stolen financial record can cause irreparable harm.

These criminals don't just seek to steal—they seek leverage.

A breach isn't just about accessing data; it's about using that data to extract ransom, control narratives, or disrupt trust.

For affluent families, the problem is compounded by the inherent trust placed in others.

Family offices rely on a network of individuals to manage assets, oversee investments, and handle personal affairs.

But every additional person increases the risk.

An employee's misstep—clicking a malicious link or reusing a weak password—can set off a chain reaction that compromises the entire network.

Even well-meaning advisors can become unintentional conduits for cybercriminals.

The consequences of a breach go beyond the immediate financial loss.

For a family office, a cyberattack can dismantle years of carefully built trust with stakeholders, investors, and even within the family itself.

A breach has the power to expose more than just bank account numbers; it can reveal personal conversations, health records, or sensitive details about business ventures.

Once exposed, that data is often irretrievable, and the fallout can last for years.

Wealth also brings a sense of invincibility that cybercriminals know how to exploit.

Many affluent families assume they are immune to cyber threats because they are careful or because they have invested in physical security.

But in the digital age, it's not the gates or the cameras that protect wealth—it's the encryption, the firewalls, and the vigilance of every individual connected to the network.

What makes wealthy families so appealing is not just what they own, but how they operate.

The layers of complexity within a family office—spanning multiple accounts, international holdings, and diverse investments—mean that even a small crack in the system can provide criminals with enough access to create chaos.

Once inside, cybercriminals move quietly, observing patterns, gathering data, and escalating their reach.

They are patient, often waiting months to strike at the most opportune moment.

This isn't just a technology problem; it's a human problem.

Cybercriminals rely on human behaviour—our habits, our shortcuts, our moments of distraction.

They exploit the trust we place in familiar names and the urgency we feel to respond quickly to requests.

They thrive on assumptions, that an email from a colleague must be legitimate, that a link from a trusted advisor is safe, that a quick decision will resolve a problem.

For family offices, the challenge lies in recognising that wealth doesn't just attract attention; it demands protection.

Cybersecurity isn't a passive safeguard; it's an active strategy.

It requires more than just software—it requires a mindset shift.

It's about understanding that the risks are personal, the stakes are high, and the attackers are relentless.

Wealthy families are high-value targets because of what they represent, opportunity.

Cybercriminals see them not as untouchable but as underprepared.

They see the gaps between privacy and security, between trust and verification, and they exploit those gaps with precision.

In the digital age, the cost of being unprepared is immeasurable.

Chapter 4 - Lessons from Real Cyber Attacks

In the shadowy world of cybercrime, real-life stories often carry the sharpest lessons.

They reveal just how vulnerable even the wealthiest and most well-guarded families can be.

These breaches aren't isolated incidents; they are part of a growing trend that targets the very people who once believed their wealth and influence could shield them.

Each case is a wake-up call, a stark reminder that in the digital world, no one is untouchable.

A family office managing billions thought their systems were airtight.

Their mistake?

Assuming trust could replace verification.

An attacker, posing as a trusted advisor, sent a carefully crafted email with an urgent request for a wire transfer.

The assistant handling the email, flustered by the pressure, complied without hesitation.

Within hours, $4 million disappeared into an untraceable offshore account.

It took weeks to uncover the breach, but the money—and the illusion of security—were gone forever.

In another case, a high-profile family found their private lives splashed across the internet.

Cybercriminals infiltrated their smart home system, gaining access to security camera footage, personal conversations, and sensitive financial documents.

The cybercriminals didn't stop there.

They threatened to release the material unless a ransom was paid.

The family complied, fearing public exposure more than the financial loss.

Even after the ransom was delivered, some of the stolen data appeared online.

The breach left the family not only financially scarred but also deeply shaken.

One of the most chilling breaches involved a prominent philanthropist whose generosity made them a visible target.

Cybercriminals spent months gathering intelligence, piecing together their digital footprint from social media, news articles, and public filings.

When the attack came, it was surgical.

The cybercriminals sent a convincing email from what appeared to be the philanthropist's charity, asking for an updated password to resolve an "account issue."

Believing it was legitimate, the philanthropist complied.

Within hours, the cybercriminals had access to financial accounts and donor records.

They drained funds and leaked private correspondence, leaving the philanthropist scrambling to rebuild trust with donors and the public.

Not all breaches are about money.

A global business leader with ties to a family office faced a sophisticated attack that exposed confidential merger talks.

Cybercriminals intercepted emails and leaked strategic plans to competitors, causing the deal to collapse.

The fallout rippled through their personal and professional lives, with investors questioning their judgment and partners doubting their ability to maintain confidentiality.

The breach wasn't just a financial hit—it was a reputational one, and it took years to recover.

Sometimes, the breach isn't high-tech.

An insider at a luxury management firm used their position to gather sensitive information on clients, including addresses, financial records, and even travel plans.

They sold this information to cybercriminals, who used it to stage targeted phishing attacks.

One family lost millions when they transferred funds to what they believed was a legitimate investment account.

It was only after the funds vanished that they discovered the breach had started with someone they trusted implicitly.

These stories aren't about carelessness; they're about overconfidence in systems that appeared secure.

Cybercriminals thrive on the belief that "it won't happen to us."

They exploit the blind spots, the unguarded moments, and the assumptions that wealth equals protection.

The reality is stark, cybercriminals don't care about status or success.

They care about access, and for wealthy families, the stakes couldn't be higher.

The aftermath of a breach is often more damaging than the attack itself.

Financial recovery is one thing, but repairing reputations, rebuilding trust, and restoring a sense of safety takes years.

For family offices, the cost isn't just measured in dollars—it's measured in relationships, opportunities, and peace of mind.

What these breaches reveal is that the playbook for cybercrime is always evolving.

Cybercriminals adapt, innovate, and exploit vulnerabilities that no one saw coming.

They know where to look, who to target, and how to wait.

Their patience is their weapon, and their targets often don't see them coming until it's too late.

These lessons are hard-earned, but they don't have to be yours.

Every breach carries a warning, vigilance isn't optional, and complacency is an open invitation.

The stories may feel distant, but the risks are closer than ever.

The question isn't if you'll be targeted—it's when.

And when that moment comes, the best defence is preparation.

Without it, the cost could be everything you've worked to protect.

Action Plan:

1. **Identify Common Threats:**
    - Research phishing, ransomware, social engineering, and insider threats.
    - Discuss real-world case studies to highlight vulnerabilities.

2. **Understand Targeted Risks:**
    - Assess how your family office's wealth, reputation, and influence make you a target.
    - Identify specific threats based on your unique operations (e.g., frequent travel, complex vendor networks).

3. **Build Awareness:**
    - Share information on current threats with family members and staff.
    - Encourage vigilance and skepticism toward unexpected emails or requests.

Checklist:

- ☐ Conduct a threat overview session with your team.
- ☐ Compile a list of potential threats tailored to your operations.
- ☐ Share examples of recent cyber incidents relevant to family offices.

Section 2

Assessing the Risks

Chapter 5 - Identifying Vulnerabilities

Cybersecurity is not just about reacting to threats; it's about knowing where they might strike before they do.

For wealthy families and family offices, identifying vulnerabilities is the foundation of a strong defence.

Cybercriminals don't look for what's secure.

They hunt for what's overlooked, what's easy to exploit, and what you think isn't a risk.

They thrive on the assumption that a system is "good enough."

But in today's world, good enough rarely is.

Mapping the threats begins with a hard look at the digital and operational systems you rely on every day.

Think of every email sent, every document stored, every device connected to your network.

Each one represents a potential doorway for a hacker.

Some of these doorways are locked, others barely latched, and a few might be wide open.

The goal is to find them all before someone else does.

Start with the basics, passwords.

They're the keys to your digital kingdom, yet they're often the weakest link.

Reused or easily guessed passwords are an open invitation for cybercriminals.

If you're using "Wealth123" or "FamilyOffice2023," you might as well hand them a map to your vault.

Strong, unique passwords are your first line of defence, but too often, they're treated as an afterthought.

Then there's email.

Every phishing attack begins with a simple click.

Cybercriminals send messages that look legitimate, often mimicking trusted contacts or organisations.

The moment someone clicks on the wrong link, the hacker gains access.

It's not about intelligence; it's about awareness.

Even the most experienced executives have been tricked by a well-crafted email.

The key is vigilance and training—knowing what to look for and treating every unexpected email as a potential threat.

Devices are another overlooked risk.

Smartphones, tablets, and laptops make life easier, but they also create vulnerabilities.

Public Wi-Fi, unsecured apps, and outdated software can all become entry points for cybercriminals.

Even a device left unlocked for a few moments can provide someone with enough time to compromise it.

Every device connected to your network needs the same level of security as your office systems because cybercriminals don't differentiate—they exploit.

Vendors and third-party relationships are a silent risk.

Family offices often work with a network of advisors, contractors, and service providers.

Each one has its own systems, its own vulnerabilities, and its own potential to create a weak link.

Cybercriminals often target vendors as a backdoor into their real target, you.

A breach at a law firm, an accountant's office, or an IT provider can quickly become your problem.

Ensuring that every partner you work with follows strict cybersecurity practices is essential.

Even your staff and family members can unintentionally create risks.

A well-meaning assistant might store passwords in a spreadsheet.

A family member might post a vacation photo online, revealing their location and travel plans.

These aren't malicious acts, but they are invitations for exploitation.

Cybersecurity isn't just about technology; it's about habits.

And habits can be trained.

Your network is another critical area to examine.

Cybercriminals often scan for unsecured networks, looking for weaknesses they can exploit.

A poorly configured router or a forgotten device connected to the network can serve as a gateway.

Regular audits of your network's security can catch these issues before they become problems.

Data storage is often treated as a safe haven, but it's anything but.

Files stored on cloud services or local servers are vulnerable without proper encryption.

Cybercriminals who gain access to these systems can copy, delete, or ransom your data.

Backups are essential, but so is ensuring those backups are secure.

The last thing you want is a hacker holding both your live data and your backups hostage.

The challenge in mapping threats is that vulnerabilities often hide in plain sight.

They're the tools and practices we use every day without questioning.

They're the shortcuts we take because they're convenient.

They're the assumptions we make because nothing has gone wrong—yet.

But cybersecurity isn't about waiting for something to go wrong. It's about staying ahead of those who want to make it go wrong.

Think of cybersecurity like maintaining a mansion.

You wouldn't leave a window open just because no one has broken in before.

You wouldn't hand out spare keys to people you barely know.

And you wouldn't rely on a lock installed decades ago.

Digital security is no different.

It requires constant attention, updates, and a willingness to question what's been taken for granted.

The process of identifying vulnerabilities can feel overwhelming, but it's necessary.

Start with an inventory of everything connected to your systems—devices, accounts, networks, and people.

Assess each one for potential weaknesses. Are passwords strong and unique?

Are devices encrypted and up to date?

Are staff and vendors trained to spot phishing attempts?

 Are your networks secure and monitored?

Every "no" is a vulnerability waiting to be exploited.

Once you've identified the risks, act on them.

Update passwords.

Encrypt sensitive data.

Train your staff.

Vet your vendors.

Regularly audit your systems to ensure that new vulnerabilities don't slip through the cracks.

Cybersecurity isn't a one-time fix; it's an ongoing process.

The threats evolve, and your defences must evolve with them.

The good news is that every vulnerability you address makes you a harder target.

Cybercriminals are opportunists.

They look for easy prey, for systems with obvious flaws and gaps.

By taking the time to map your threats and address your weaknesses, you force them to move on to someone else. In the world of cybercrime, preparation isn't just protection—it's power.

It's the power to stay one step ahead, to safeguard what matters most, and to ensure that the story of your family office isn't one of loss, but one of resilience.

Chapter 6 - Protecting Non-Financial Assets

When most people think about cybercrime, they imagine stolen bank accounts, fraudulent wire transfers, or drained investment portfolios.

But for wealthy families and their offices, the stakes go far beyond the numbers.

In today's digital world, intellectual property, family privacy, and reputations are as valuable—and as vulnerable—as any financial asset.

Cybercriminals know this, and they target these intangible assets with the same precision and persistence they use to steal money.

Imagine this, confidential emails revealing private family disputes leaked to the press, causing a public relations nightmare.

Or cybercriminals intercepting plans for a billion-dollar acquisition, leaking the details to competitors and derailing the deal.

These aren't hypotheticals.

They've happened, and they'll happen again.

Financial loss is one thing, but the cost of a damaged reputation or stolen intellectual property can last for years.

Intellectual property is often overlooked in cybersecurity discussions, yet it's one of the most sought-after targets.

Family offices managing diverse portfolios often hold the blueprints to new inventions, business strategies, or proprietary methods.

Cybercriminals see this as a jackpot.

Once stolen, these assets can be sold to competitors or leaked to the public, wiping out competitive advantages built over decades.

The more innovative or influential your business dealings, the more attractive you are as a target.

Family privacy is another area where cybercriminals excel at causing harm.

It doesn't take much for a hacker to dig into personal details—addresses, travel schedules, medical records, or even private photos.

The wealthier the family, the more value such information holds.

Criminals know they can sell it, use it to extort, or simply release it to the public for notoriety.

The fallout is often personal and devastating, eroding trust and safety in spaces meant to be private.

Your reputation, however, might be the most fragile asset of all.

In the digital world, reputations are built and broken in an instant.

A single leak of sensitive emails or documents can go viral, casting doubt on your integrity and leadership.

Cybercriminals don't just want to steal from you; they want to destabilise you.

They understand that for high-profile families and businesses, public perception is priceless.

The threat of losing it can force victims into paying ransoms or complying with other demands.

The challenge with protecting non-financial assets is that they're everywhere and often intangible.

Financial accounts can be monitored with clear safeguards like encryption and multi-factor authentication.

But how do you protect an idea?

A private conversation?

A family's good name?

These assets are harder to quantify, yet the damage from losing them is immeasurable.

Cybercriminals exploit this lack of clarity.

They know that many wealthy families haven't considered the full extent of their vulnerabilities.

They also know that the more discreet and private you try to be, the less likely you are to seek external help.

That secrecy is what they count on.

It gives them the space they need to act without detection.

Protecting these assets requires a shift in mindset.

It's no longer enough to focus on money and accounts. You must think about every piece of data, every conversation, and every interaction as a potential target.

Intellectual property, family privacy, and reputation don't live in silos.

They're woven into the fabric of how family offices operate.

Every email, meeting, and document carries traces of them, and every trace is an opportunity for exploitation.

Start with intellectual property.

Map out what's most valuable, whether it's trade secrets, patents, or proprietary processes.

Secure these assets as rigorously as you would secure your financial data.

Limit access to only those who need it, and monitor how it's shared.

Encryption is key, but so is educating those who handle it.

The fewer hands it passes through, the safer it stays.

For family privacy, the goal is control.

Control over who knows what, who can access it, and how it's stored.

Personal data should be treated with the same caution as financial records.

Encrypt medical files. Avoid sharing travel plans publicly.

Secure home networks with the same intensity as your office systems.

Even something as simple as a smart home device can become a vulnerability if left unprotected.

Cybercriminals have used connected devices to spy on families, listening to conversations or watching through security cameras.

Every connected device is a potential window into your life.

Keep them locked.

Reputation requires proactive vigilance.

Assume that every email, text, or document could one day be leaked.

Operate with a level of professionalism that minimises the damage if it happens.

Don't send sensitive information over unsecured channels, and don't say anything in writing you wouldn't want on the front page of tomorrow's paper.

Reputation isn't just about what you say; it's about how you behave.

Cybercriminals will look for the smallest indiscretions to amplify, so don't give them the ammunition.

The digital world has changed the rules of wealth management.

Non-financial assets are no longer secondary.

They are primary targets, and the consequences of losing them can ripple through every part of your life and business.

Cybercriminals know this, and they're betting you don't.

They exploit not just technical vulnerabilities but also gaps in awareness and preparation.

For family offices, protecting non-financial assets isn't just a technical exercise; it's a cultural one.

It's about embedding cybersecurity into every aspect of how you operate, from how you communicate to how you think.

Intellectual property, family privacy, and reputation may seem intangible, but they're as real—and as valuable—as any bank account.

In many ways, they're even more critical because they define who you are and what you stand for.

The time to act is before these assets are threatened, not after.

Cybercriminals are counting on you to focus only on the obvious while they go after everything else.

Don't let them win. In the digital age, your most important assets can't be seen, but they must be protected.

Chapter 7 - Inside-Out Risks,

The greatest threats often come from within. In the world of cybersecurity, insider threats are the risks you never see coming until it's too late.

It's not just cybercriminals on the outside you need to worry about—it's the people you trust most on the inside.

Staff, vendors, and even family members can unintentionally, or sometimes maliciously, expose your most sensitive information.

These risks are harder to spot, more difficult to prevent, and can cause devastating harm.

Imagine an assistant forwarding a confidential email to the wrong person.

A vendor using outdated systems that let cybercriminals in through a side door.

A family member sharing too much on social media, revealing schedules or sensitive travel plans.

None of these actions seem malicious, yet their consequences can be catastrophic.

Cybercriminals don't need to break in when someone on the inside has already left the door wide open.

The challenge with insider threats is their invisibility.

People rarely mean to cause harm, but their mistakes can have far-reaching consequences.

A misplaced file, a weak password, or a casual conversation in public can create opportunities for cybercriminals.

Cybercriminals know this, and they exploit human error at every turn.

They count on people being busy, distracted, or overly trusting.

These lapses are their golden opportunities.

Some insider threats, however, aren't accidental.

Disgruntled employees, unhappy vendors, or even family disputes can create deliberate risks.

A staff member who feels undervalued might leak sensitive data out of spite.

A vendor with lax security might become a conduit for attackers.

Even trusted family members, under pressure or in conflict, could make choices that expose your vulnerabilities.

These scenarios may seem unlikely, but they happen more often than anyone likes to admit.

The problem with insider threats is that they're personal.

It's not just systems and protocols being compromised—it's relationships.

When someone close to you, intentionally or not, becomes the source of a breach, it shakes the very foundation of trust.

The fallout goes beyond financial loss.

It damages morale, disrupts operations, and often creates long-lasting tensions.

Managing these risks requires a balance of vigilance and empathy.

People are not machines.

They make mistakes, act on emotions, and occasionally cut corners.

The key is to build a culture of awareness, accountability, and prevention.

It's about creating an environment where risks are recognised and addressed without breeding fear or suspicion.

Start by understanding who has access to what.

Not everyone in your organisation needs access to every system, file, or piece of information.

Limit permissions based on roles, and regularly review who has access to critical assets.

If someone leaves the organisation or changes roles, their access should change too.

Many breaches occur simply because outdated access wasn't revoked.

Education is your next line of defence.

Most insider risks stem from a lack of awareness, not malice.

Teach your staff, vendors, and even family members about the risks they face and the role they play in keeping your systems secure.

Simple practices, like recognising phishing attempts, using strong passwords, and verifying unexpected requests, can go a long way in preventing mistakes.

At the same time, it's crucial to monitor activity within your systems.

Unusual behaviour, like large file downloads, repeated login failures, or access attempts outside normal hours, can signal an insider threat.

Monitoring doesn't mean mistrust—it's about ensuring that any potential issues are caught early before they escalate.

Vendors pose a unique challenge.

They are an essential part of your operation, but they also introduce risks.

When you work with external partners, you're entrusting them with access to your network, your data, and sometimes your reputation.

Vetting vendors for strong cybersecurity practices is non-negotiable.

Insist on clear agreements that outline how they will protect your data and what steps they will take if they're breached.

Don't just take their word for it—verify their practices regularly.

Family members, too, need guidance.

It's easy to assume that those closest to you won't pose a risk, but their habits and behaviours can create vulnerabilities.

A family member who clicks on a phishing email, uses a weak password, or discusses private matters in a public space can inadvertently cause harm.

Educate them about these risks without making them feel scrutinised.

The goal is to empower them to be part of the solution.

For intentional insider threats, prevention lies in fostering a culture where grievances are addressed openly, not left to fester.

Discontented employees are more likely to act out if they feel unheard or undervalued.

Regular check-ins, clear communication, and fair treatment can reduce the likelihood of malicious behaviour.

When someone does leave the organisation, ensure their access is immediately revoked, and any potential risks they pose are mitigated.

No system is perfect, but managing insider threats is about reducing opportunities for mistakes and misconduct.

It's about creating layers of protection that make it harder for vulnerabilities to be exploited.

The strongest defences are built on trust, awareness, and preparation.

Insider threats are often the hardest to anticipate because they come from places of familiarity.

But familiarity shouldn't breed complacency.

The people you trust with your operations are also the people you trust with your risks.

Recognising this is not about suspicion—it's about responsibility.

In the end, protecting against insider threats isn't just about safeguarding your systems.

It's about safeguarding the relationships, reputations, and legacies that those systems represent.

Trust is vital, but trust alone isn't enough. It must be matched with vigilance and action.

Chapter 8 - The Ripple Effect!

Cybercrime doesn't just steal money; it steals trust, confidence, and the foundation on which legacies are built.

For wealthy families, a single breach can send shockwaves through everything they've worked to create.

The damage isn't confined to bank accounts—it reaches far deeper, disrupting generational wealth transfer, damaging reputations, and dismantling the trust that holds everything together.

Imagine decades of careful planning wiped out in moments.

A hacker gains access to sensitive financial documents and releases them online.

Suddenly, private details about family investments and philanthropic plans become public.

Competitors swoop in, business deals fall apart, and the family's carefully crafted public image takes a hit.

It's not just about money lost—it's about control, influence, and the ability to shape the future.

The ripple effect starts small.

A single point of failure—a compromised email account, a leaked password, or an unguarded conversation—sets off a chain reaction.

What begins as a breach quickly escalates into a crisis.

Confidential communications are exposed, trust among family members erodes, and once-secure relationships with advisors and partners are strained.

Every layer of the family office feels the impact, from daily operations to long-term strategy.

The impact on generational wealth transfer is particularly devastating.

Families often spend years crafting intricate plans to ensure wealth moves seamlessly from one generation to the next.

Cybercrime disrupts these plans in ways no one expects.

If financial accounts are compromised, assets can be stolen or mismanaged before the family even realises what's happened.

Worse, the reputational fallout can create lingering doubts about the family's ability to protect its legacy.

Heirs and stakeholders may lose faith in the systems designed to preserve their future.

Reputation is another casualty of cybercrime.

In the digital age, reputations are fragile, built on trust and the perception of security.

A breach doesn't just expose data—it exposes vulnerability.

When a family office is hacked, it sends a signal to the world, "They weren't prepared."

This perception can damage relationships with investors, donors, and partners.

It can make it harder to negotiate deals, attract talent, or maintain influence.

Reputation, once lost, is incredibly hard to regain, and cybercriminals know this.

They often exploit the fear of public exposure as a tool to demand ransom or manipulate victims.

Trust, once broken, ripples outward. Within families, a breach can sow seeds of doubt.

Did someone make a mistake? Was it preventable?

Who is responsible?

These questions linger, creating tension where once there was unity.

External relationships suffer too.

Advisors, vendors, and partners may question the family office's ability to safeguard sensitive information.

This doubt can lead to lost opportunities, as partners hesitate to engage with an entity they perceive as a risk.

The ripple effect doesn't stop there.

It reaches philanthropic efforts, disrupting charitable initiatives and tarnishing the family's public image.

Donors and beneficiaries alike may distance themselves, fearing association with a compromised organisation.

The loss isn't just financial—it's a loss of impact, influence, and the ability to shape the world in meaningful ways.

Cybercrime's true cost lies in its ability to unravel what has been built over generations.

Wealth is more than money—it's trust, reputation, and the ability to leave a lasting mark.

A breach threatens all of this, creating a legacy not of success but of vulnerability.

The good news is that the ripple effect can be stopped.

Awareness is the first step. Understanding the stakes makes it clear that cybersecurity is not just a technical concern—it's a fundamental part of wealth and legacy management.

Preparation is the second step.

Building robust defences, training staff, and regularly auditing systems can reduce the chances of a breach.

Finally, response matters.

When a breach happens, acting swiftly and decisively can contain the damage and prevent further fallout.

Cybercrime is not just a threat to the present—it's a threat to the future.

The ripple effect reminds us that every decision made today impacts what's left for tomorrow.

Wealthy families must understand this reality, confront it, and act.

Because in the end, protecting wealth isn't just about numbers—it's about securing the trust, reputation, and legacy that make it truly valuable

Action Plan:

1. **Map Your Digital Assets:**
   - List all devices, networks, software, and data your office uses.
   - Identify who has access to each resource.

2. **Evaluate Existing Defences:**
   - Audit passwords, encryption, and access controls.
   - Check for outdated software or unpatched systems.

3. **Review Insider Risks:**
   - Assess risks from staff, vendors, and family members.
   - Monitor access and activity logs for unusual behaviour.

4. **Assess Data Sensitivity:**
   - Identify and prioritise protecting high-value information such as financial records, personal data, and intellectual property.

Checklist:

- [ ] Conduct a full digital and operational audit.
- [ ] Implement strong password policies and two-factor authentication.
- [ ] Review staff training and vendor security standards.
- [ ] Encrypt sensitive files and communications.

Section 3

Building Your Defence

Chapter 9 - Cyber Hygiene 101.

Cybersecurity isn't just about high-tech systems and complex defences.

It starts with the basics—simple, everyday habits that keep your family and your systems safe.

These small steps, when done consistently, build a powerful first line of defence.

Cybercriminals thrive on mistakes, and good cyber hygiene is about eliminating those mistakes before they happen.

Strong passwords are your digital keys, yet they're often the weakest link.

Cybercriminals can crack simple passwords like "123456" or "password" in seconds.

Avoid reusing the same password across multiple accounts.

Instead, use unique passwords for each account and store them in a password manager.

A strong password is at least 12 characters long and includes letters, numbers, and symbols.

Think of it as a lock that grows stronger with every added layer.

Two-factor authentication is the next essential step.

This adds an extra layer of security by requiring a second form of verification, like a code sent to your phone or an app.

Even if a hacker steals your password, they can't get in without the second factor.

Enable it wherever possible, especially for email, banking, and social media accounts.

It's a simple step that can stop a breach in its tracks.

Phishing emails remain one of the most common ways cybercriminals get inside.

They look legitimate, often mimicking trusted contacts or companies, but they're designed to trick you.

Be cautious with any email asking you to click a link or provide personal information.

Verify the sender before acting. Hover over links to check where they lead.

If something feels off, trust your instincts.

Cybercriminals rely on quick reactions—slow down and think before you click.

Your devices are another critical point of entry.

Keep your software up to date.

Updates fix vulnerabilities that cybercriminals love to exploit.

Enable automatic updates on all devices, including computers, phones, and tablets.

 Use antivirus software and run regular scans.

Encrypt sensitive files and back up your data to a secure location.

If a device is lost or stolen, remote wipe features can protect your information.

Public Wi-Fi may seem convenient, but it's a hacker's playground.

Avoid using public networks for anything sensitive, like banking or accessing your email.

If you must use public Wi-Fi, connect through a virtual private network (VPN).

A VPN creates a secure, encrypted tunnel between your device and the internet, making it much harder for cybercriminals to intercept your data.

Smart home devices add convenience, but they also create risks.

Each device—whether it's a thermostat, a security camera, or a smart speaker—is another entry point for cybercriminals.

Change default passwords on these devices, and keep their software up to date.

Segment your home network so smart devices are isolated from sensitive systems.

A hacker gaining access to your smart lightbulbs shouldn't give them access to your financial accounts.

Social media is another area where good hygiene matters.

Think twice before sharing details about your location, travel plans, or purchases.

Cybercriminals use this information to profile you and plan attacks.

Tighten your privacy settings to limit what strangers can see.

What seems like harmless sharing can provide cybercriminals with valuable clues.

Family members and staff need to follow these practices too.

Cybersecurity is a team effort, and one weak link can compromise everyone.

Provide training on the basics of phishing, password management, and device security.

Make cybersecurity part of the family's routine, not an afterthought.

Regularly remind everyone why these habits matter. Awareness is the best defence.

Backup plans aren't just for emergencies—they're essential.

Regularly back up important data to a secure, offline location.

If ransomware locks your systems, you'll have a clean copy to restore.

Test your backups to ensure they work.

Losing access to data can be as disruptive as losing the data itself.

Monitor your accounts and systems for unusual activity.

Many breaches go unnoticed because no one is watching.

Set up alerts for suspicious logins or changes to your accounts.

Review bank and credit card statements regularly for signs of fraud.

Early detection can prevent a small problem from becoming a big one.

Good cyber hygiene doesn't require advanced technical skills.

It's about forming habits that make you less of a target.

Cybercriminals prefer easy prey.

By taking these simple steps, you make their job harder.

Consistency is key.

Just as you lock your doors at night without thinking, these practices should become second nature.

The digital world is filled with risks, but it's also filled with opportunities to protect yourself.

Cyber hygiene is about taking control, staying aware, and acting before threats become problems.

For families and family offices, it's the foundation of security.

Strong defences begin with small, deliberate actions.

Don't wait for a breach to realise their importance.

Start today.

Chapter 10 - Cybersecurity, A Tailored Approach

Cybersecurity for family offices isn't about following generic advice.

It's about creating a system that fits the unique way you operate, protects the wealth you manage, and shields the trust you've built.

Cybercriminals know family offices are different from corporations.

They also know many are underprepared.

A tailored approach to cybersecurity can stop them before they even begin.

Start by understanding what's at stake.

Family offices don't just handle money—they manage legacies, reputations, and the relationships that hold everything together.

A breach isn't just a technical issue. It's personal, and it's often devastating.

Your cybersecurity strategy needs to reflect this reality.

It has to protect not just your systems but the trust that defines your work.

Begin with a clear view of your risks.

Map out every system, device, and network your office relies on.

Every email account, cloud storage service, and file-sharing platform is a potential entry point for cybercriminals.

Once you have this map, assess the security of each element.

Are passwords strong and unique?

Is sensitive data encrypted?

Are systems patched and updated regularly?

A comprehensive audit will show you where you're vulnerable and where to focus your efforts.

Access control is one of the most effective ways to reduce risk.

Not everyone needs access to everything.

Limit permissions based on roles and responsibilities.

A junior assistant doesn't need the same access as a senior advisor.

When someone leaves or their role changes, revoke or adjust their access immediately.

Cybercriminals often exploit outdated permissions to find their way in.

Staff training is essential.

Most breaches start with human error—a click on a phishing link, a weak password, or a careless moment.

Regular training sessions can help your team spot threats and respond appropriately.

Teach them to recognise phishing attempts, use two-factor authentication, and handle sensitive data securely.

Make cybersecurity training an ongoing process, not a one-time event.

Vendors are another critical area to address.

Your family office likely works with a range of third parties, from accountants to IT providers.

Each one introduces a new layer of risk.

Before partnering with any vendor, vet their cybersecurity practices.

Ensure they follow strict protocols for handling your data.

Include clear terms in your contracts about how they will protect your information and what happens if they are breached.

Verify their compliance regularly.

Trust is important, but verification is essential.

Monitoring is the backbone of any strong cybersecurity strategy.

Cybercriminals often spend weeks or months inside a system before launching an attack.

Early detection can stop them in their tracks.

Set up tools to monitor for unusual activity, like failed login attempts, unexpected file downloads, or access from unfamiliar locations.

These signs often indicate an intruder.

Act quickly when you see them.

The faster you respond, the less damage they can do.

Encryption is another must-have for family offices.

Sensitive data—whether it's financial records, personal correspondence, or strategic plans—should always be encrypted.

Encryption ensures that even if data is intercepted, it's unreadable without the right key.

Use encryption for files, emails, and communications.

Encourage encrypted messaging platforms for sensitive discussions.

It's a small step that adds a significant layer of protection.

A tailored approach also means preparing for the worst.

Even with the best defences, no system is invincible.

Have a plan in place for responding to a breach. Know who to call, what to do, and how to minimise the damage.

A strong incident response plan can mean the difference between a minor disruption and a major crisis.

Test your plan regularly to ensure it works when you need it most.

Investing in advanced security tools can make a big difference.

Firewalls, endpoint protection, and intrusion detection systems are essential.

But tools alone aren't enough.

Combine them with clear policies and vigilant monitoring to create a multi-layered defence.

Cybercriminals look for weak spots, and a layered approach makes it harder for them to find one.

Family offices often handle private communications that extend beyond the office itself.

Personal devices, home networks, and even smart devices can create vulnerabilities.

Ensure that family members follow the same security protocols as the office.

Require strong passwords, encrypted devices, and secure networks.

Educate them about the risks and provide them with the tools they need to stay safe.

Physical security also plays a role in cybersecurity.

A stolen laptop, an unlocked office, or a misplaced phone can provide cybercriminals with easy access.

Use secure storage for devices, lock sensitive documents in physical safes, and ensure all devices can be remotely wiped if lost or stolen.

Protecting physical assets helps safeguard digital ones too.

Ultimately, the goal of a tailored cybersecurity approach is to make your family office a hard target.

Cybercriminals prefer easy wins.

By investing in the right tools, training, and strategies, you can make their job as difficult as possible.

Strong defences don't just protect your office—they protect the wealth, reputation, and legacy you're trusted to manage.

Cybersecurity for family offices isn't optional.

It's a necessity.

The risks are real, but the solutions are within reach.

By tailoring your approach, you can build a system that doesn't just respond to threats but actively prevents them.

In the digital age, that's not just smart—it's essential.

Chapter 11 - Building Your Cyber Toolkit!

When it comes to cybersecurity, the right tools make all the difference.

Cybercriminals rely on gaps—outdated software, weak defences, and unsecured systems.

With a strong cyber toolkit, you can close those gaps and make your family office a fortress.

The tools you choose must work together to stop threats before they happen, detect them when they occur, and respond quickly if they get through.

Start with endpoint protection.

Every device—laptop, tablet, phone—is a potential target.

Endpoint protection acts as a guard at the gate, detecting and blocking threats like malware and ransomware.

Choose tools that offer real-time monitoring and updates.

Make sure all devices connected to your network, including those used by staff and family members, have this protection.

A single unsecured device can bring down an entire system.

Encryption is the backbone of modern cybersecurity.

It protects sensitive data by scrambling it into unreadable code, accessible only with the right key.

Use encryption for emails, files, and even storage devices.

If a hacker intercepts your data, encryption ensures they can't use it.

Cloud storage should also include encryption, both during transmission and at rest.

Insist on end-to-end encryption for sensitive communications to ensure privacy.

Secure communications are non-negotiable.

Email is often a weak link, easily exploited by phishing scams.

Choose email services with built-in encryption and phishing protection.

Encourage staff and family members to use encrypted messaging apps for sensitive discussions.

Tools like Signal or WhatsApp offer strong privacy features.

For video calls, choose platforms with robust encryption and secure meeting settings.

Firewalls are another must-have.

They act as your first line of defence, filtering incoming traffic to block threats before they reach your network.

A strong firewall is more than a barrier—it's a filter that learns and adapts.

Regularly update firewall settings and monitor logs for suspicious activity.

Combine firewalls with intrusion detection systems to catch attackers who try to sneak past.

Two-factor authentication adds an extra layer of security.

Even if a hacker steals your password, they can't access your accounts without a second form of verification, like a text message or app-generated code.

Enable two-factor authentication on all critical accounts, including email, banking, and cloud storage.

It's simple to set up and stops most attacks before they start.

Virtual private networks (VPNs) are essential for protecting your internet connection.

A VPN creates an encrypted tunnel between your device and the internet, hiding your activity from cybercriminals.

Use a VPN whenever you connect to public Wi-Fi or access sensitive data remotely.

Choose a trusted provider with no logging policies to ensure your privacy is protected.

For family offices managing sensitive documents, data loss prevention (DLP) tools are invaluable.

DLP software monitors data movement, ensuring files don't leave your network without proper authorisation.

It also alerts you if sensitive information, like financial records or personal details, is at risk of being exposed.

This tool provides an extra layer of oversight and control.

Password managers are a simple but powerful tool.

They generate and store strong, unique passwords for every account, eliminating the need to remember them.

A password manager reduces the risk of reused or weak passwords, one of the most common causes of breaches.

Choose a manager that encrypts your passwords and offers secure sharing options.

Network monitoring tools keep watch over your systems, flagging unusual activity in real-time.

These tools can detect threats like unauthorised logins, large data transfers, or attempts to access restricted files.

Set up alerts for suspicious behaviour and review logs regularly.

Monitoring doesn't stop attacks, but it gives you the time and information to respond quickly.

Regular backups are your safety net. Ransomware can lock you out of your data, but a secure backup ensures you won't lose everything.

Use both local and cloud backups for redundancy, and test them regularly to make sure they work. Encrypt your backups and store them securely, separate from your main systems.

In a crisis, a reliable backup can save you from disaster.

Antivirus software remains a staple of any cybersecurity toolkit.

Modern antivirus programs offer more than just virus scanning—they detect and block a wide range of threats, including spyware, ransomware, and phishing attacks.

Choose a solution that updates automatically to stay ahead of new threats.

Make antivirus scans a regular part of your routine.

For family offices with multiple locations or remote teams, secure access tools are crucial.

Virtual desktop infrastructure (VDI) allows staff to access systems without storing sensitive data on their devices.

This reduces the risk of data leaks from lost or stolen equipment.

Multi-factor authentication should be a standard feature for all remote access tools.

Physical security also integrates with digital security.

Ensure servers, routers, and storage devices are physically secured in locked rooms or cabinets.

Use cameras and access controls to monitor sensitive areas.

Physical breaches can lead to digital disasters, so protect your hardware as carefully as your software.

Your cyber toolkit is only as strong as its weakest link.

Integrate these tools into a cohesive system that works together, rather than as individual pieces.

Regularly update and audit your tools to ensure they remain effective.

Cybersecurity is not a one-time investment—it's an ongoing process of improvement and adaptation.

Cybercriminals are relentless, but they're also opportunists.

They look for easy targets, systems with gaps, and tools left unmaintained.

A strong toolkit backed by regular maintenance and vigilance makes their job harder.

For family offices, this isn't just about protecting assets—it's about protecting trust, reputation, and the legacy you're building.

The technology you choose should reflect the stakes you face.

Cybersecurity isn't optional—it's the foundation of everything you do.

With the right tools in place, you're not just defending against threats.

You're creating an environment where your family office can thrive, secure in the knowledge that its most valuable assets are protected.

Chapter 12 - Creating a Culture of Cyber Awareness

Cybersecurity isn't just about tools and systems; it's about people.

The strongest defences can fail if the people behind them aren't paying attention.

Cybercriminals know this. They exploit habits, emotions, and simple mistakes to get inside.

Creating a culture of cyber awareness isn't optional—it's the foundation of your defence.

Start by making cybersecurity personal.

People care more when they understand how threats affect their lives.

Show them how phishing scams, weak passwords, or oversharing online can lead to stolen identities, leaked data, or financial loss.

Use real examples to make the risks feel real.

When the stakes are clear, people take action.

Training isn't a one-time event.

It needs to be part of your routine.

Teach staff, family members, and board members how to spot phishing attempts, create strong passwords, and use tools like two-factor authentication.

Break it down into simple steps they can follow every day.

Short, focused sessions are more effective than long lectures.

Keep it interactive with quizzes, exercises, or simulations.

When people practice, they remember.

Engage everyone in the process.

Cybersecurity isn't just for IT teams—it's everyone's responsibility.

Make sure staff know they play a critical role in keeping systems secure.

Involve family members by showing them how to protect their personal devices and online activities.

Help board members understand the strategic importance of cybersecurity for the family office.

When everyone feels involved, they're more likely to stay engaged.

Use stories to drive your message home.

Share examples of real attacks, especially ones that show how simple mistakes can have big consequences.

A missed warning sign, a click on a malicious link, or a casual conversation in public—these small actions can lead to huge problems.

Stories make abstract risks concrete, helping people connect with the issue on a deeper level.

Reinforce good habits every chance you get.

Post reminders about phishing red flags near workstations.

Send monthly emails with quick tips on staying safe online.

Celebrate when someone spots and reports a phishing attempt.

Positive reinforcement builds momentum.

Over time, good habits become second nature.

Build a system of accountability.

Cyber awareness isn't about blame—it's about responsibility.

Make it clear that everyone is expected to follow security protocols.

Regularly check that passwords are strong, updates are installed, and suspicious emails are reported.

If someone slips up, use it as a learning moment, not a punishment.

Accountability works best when it's paired with support.

Leaders set the tone.

When executives and board members take cybersecurity seriously, it sends a message to everyone else.

Show your commitment by attending training sessions, asking questions about security plans, and following best practices yourself.

Actions speak louder than words, and visible leadership makes a difference.

Regularly update your approach.

Cyber threats evolve, and so should your training. Stay informed about new scams, tactics, and tools.

Share updates with your team and adapt your training to address emerging risks.

A culture of awareness isn't static—it grows and changes with the threat landscape.

Use technology to make awareness easier.

Tools like phishing simulators can help staff practice spotting fake emails.

Password managers reduce the stress of creating and remembering strong passwords.

Cybersecurity tools are important, but their real value comes when people know how to use them effectively.

Foster an open environment where people feel comfortable asking questions or reporting concerns.

Cybersecurity can be intimidating, especially for those who aren't tech-savvy.

Make it clear that no question is too small and no mistake is beyond fixing.

When people feel safe speaking up, they're more likely to act quickly and honestly if they notice something suspicious.

Cyber awareness doesn't end at the office.

Encourage family members to apply the same principles at home.

Show them how to secure their Wi-Fi networks, avoid oversharing on social media, and protect their devices while traveling.

The line between personal and professional security is blurry, especially for family offices.

A breach at home can lead to problems at work.

Celebrate progress.

A culture of cyber awareness takes time to build, and every step forward is worth recognising.

Highlight successes, like avoided phishing attempts or completed training sessions.

Share stories of how awareness made a difference.

Celebrate these moments to keep the momentum going.

The goal isn't perfection—it's progress. Cyber threats will always exist, but with the right mindset, you can reduce the risks.

A culture of awareness turns your people from potential weak links into active defenders. It makes cybersecurity a shared responsibility, not a solo effort.

Cybercriminals thrive on carelessness, complacency, and confusion. A strong culture of awareness takes those advantages away. It creates a team that's vigilant, informed, and ready to act.

In today's digital world, that's not just valuable—it's essential. Cybersecurity isn't just about what you do—it's about who you are.

Make awareness part of your identity, and you'll create a defence no hacker can break.

Action Plan:

1. **Strengthen Defences:**
    - Invest in endpoint protection, firewalls, and monitoring tools.
    - Use encryption for emails, files, and backups.

2. **Implement Secure Practices:**
    - Train staff and family members in recognising phishing and other scams.
    - Regularly update all devices and software.

3. **Create a Response Plan:**
    - Develop a step-by-step guide for handling breaches.
    - Include clear roles, communication protocols, and recovery steps.

4. **Foster Awareness:**
    - Run regular cybersecurity workshops.
    - Reward employees for spotting and preventing potential breaches.

Checklist:

- [ ] Install and maintain advanced cybersecurity tools (firewalls, antivirus, monitoring).
- [ ] Implement two-factor authentication on all accounts.
- [ ] Conduct regular staff training and phishing simulations.
- [ ] Test and refine your incident response plan.

Section 4

Advanced Defence Strategies

Chapter 13 - Staying One Step Ahead!

Cybercrime doesn't announce itself with a loud crash or flashing lights.

It slips in quietly, waits, watches, and strikes when you least expect it.

Cybercriminals don't just break in—they linger.

They learn your patterns, explore your systems, and take their time finding what's most valuable.

That's why monitoring and response are not optional.

They are the cornerstones of staying one step ahead.

Monitoring gives you the eyes and ears to detect threats in real time.

Cybercriminals leave digital traces as they move through systems—unusual logins, sudden spikes in data transfers, or access from strange locations.

Advanced monitoring tools spot these signs instantly, flagging potential breaches before they become disasters.

Without these tools, you're blind, unaware of what's happening until it's too late.

Start with your network.

Install monitoring systems that track every device and connection.

Look for tools that alert you to unusual activity, like multiple failed login attempts or access from unfamiliar locations.

These anomalies are often the first sign of trouble.

A proactive approach means you can respond before cybercriminals can do serious damage.

Endpoint detection is equally critical.

Every phone, laptop, and tablet connected to your network is a potential entry point for attackers.

Advanced endpoint tools monitor these devices in real time, spotting malware, phishing attempts, and other threats.

They don't just block attacks—they provide detailed logs that help you understand what happened and how to prevent it in the future.

Response plans are your safety net.

No system is perfect, and even the best defences can fail.

What matters is how quickly and effectively you respond.

Create a clear incident response plan that outlines exactly what to do when a breach occurs.

Who will you call?

What steps will you take?

How will you minimise the damage?

A good plan turns chaos into control.

Test your response plan regularly.

Simulate breaches to see how your team reacts.

Identify weaknesses in your process and fix them before a real attack happens.

Practice makes the difference between a contained incident and a full-blown crisis.

Every second counts when dealing with cybercrime, and a practiced team can save valuable time.

Automation is your ally in staying ahead.

Manual monitoring and response can't keep up with the speed of modern attacks.

Automated systems analyse data in real time, flagging threats instantly and even taking initial action, like isolating compromised devices.

This buys you time to assess and act.

Look for tools that integrate seamlessly with your existing systems and provide clear, actionable insights.

Monitoring doesn't stop at the network level.

Keep an eye on the dark web for stolen data or credentials linked to your family office.

Cybercriminals often sell this information long before you realise it's been stolen.

Services exist to scan these spaces, alerting you to potential risks before they escalate.

Knowing your data is out there gives you the chance to act—change passwords, shut down compromised accounts, or alert relevant authorities.

Communication is key during a response.

In the heat of an incident, clear and concise communication keeps everyone on the same page.

Establish a protocol for who needs to be informed and how updates will be shared.

Miscommunication can waste precious time and lead to mistakes.

Your response team should know their roles and have the tools to coordinate effectively.

Don't forget about recovery.

A breach isn't over once the threat is neutralised.

You need to assess what was affected, restore systems, and implement fixes to prevent future attacks.

Backup systems play a crucial role here.

Regularly updated, secure backups ensure you can restore operations quickly without paying ransoms or losing critical data.

Transparency builds trust.

After an incident, communicate openly with stakeholders, including family members, staff, and partners.

Share what happened, what steps you took, and how you're improving your defences.

Silence breeds suspicion, but honesty shows you're in control and committed to protecting your assets.

Monitoring and response are ongoing processes.

Cybercriminals evolve, and so must your defences.

Regularly update your tools, review your plans, and adapt to new threats.

Staying one step ahead requires constant vigilance and a willingness to invest in the right systems.

Cybercriminals count on complacency.

They look for organisations that assume they're safe because nothing has happened yet.

Monitoring and response prove them wrong.

By watching your systems, acting quickly, and learning from every incident, you build a defence that's as dynamic as the threats you face.

In the end, the best defence isn't just about blocking attacks—it's about knowing what's happening and responding before it's too late.

Cybercrime moves fast, but with the right tools and strategies, you can move faster.

Monitoring and response are your edge.

Use them well, and you'll stay ahead, no matter what comes your way.

Chapter 14 - Cyber Resilience.

No system is perfect.

Even with the strongest defences, breaches can happen.

Cyber resilience isn't about hoping you won't be attacked—it's about preparing for when you are.

It's about staying calm under pressure, acting quickly, and keeping your family office running when chaos strikes.

Imagine waking up to find your systems locked, your data stolen, or your reputation under fire.

Without a plan, panic sets in.

With a plan, you know what to do.

Resilience starts with a clear, tested incident response plan.

This plan is your blueprint for action when the worst happens.

It outlines who does what, when, and how. It turns confusion into control.

An effective incident response plan begins with roles.

Assign a response team and make sure everyone knows their responsibilities.

Who will assess the damage?

Who will notify key stakeholders?

Who will communicate with vendors, partners, or even the media?

Clear roles eliminate delays and prevent missteps during critical moments.

Next, create a step-by-step process for handling a breach.

Start with containment. Identify the affected systems, isolate them from the network, and stop the threat from spreading.

Then assess the damage.

What was accessed?

What was stolen?

What needs to be restored?

Finally, focus on recovery.

Bring systems back online, secure vulnerabilities, and communicate the steps you're taking to prevent a repeat.

Testing your plan is as important as creating it.

Simulate a breach and run through your response.

Practice reveals gaps in the plan and gives your team the confidence to act quickly under pressure.

Update the plan regularly to reflect new risks, tools, or team changes.

A plan that sits untouched in a drawer won't help when you need it most.

Business continuity is the second pillar of resilience.

Cyberattacks can disrupt your operations, but they don't have to shut you down.

A business continuity plan ensures that critical functions continue even during a crisis.

It starts with identifying what's essential.

Which systems, processes, and data are vital to your family office?

Prioritise these in your recovery efforts.

Backups are your safety net.

Regularly back up all critical data and test those backups to make sure they work.

Store backups securely, both on-site and in the cloud.

If ransomware locks your systems, a reliable backup can save you from paying a ransom or losing important information.

Communication is key during a crisis.

A well-crafted communication plan keeps everyone informed and focused. Know who needs to be notified, what they need to know, and how to deliver the message.

Be honest and transparent with stakeholders.

A clear explanation of what happened, what you're doing, and how you'll prevent future issues builds trust even in difficult times.

Vendor relationships matter, too.

A breach at one of your partners can impact your operations.

Include them in your continuity planning.

Ask how they'll support you during a crisis and ensure they have their own incident response and recovery plans in place.

Trust is important, but verification ensures readiness.

Resilience also means learning from every incident.

After the crisis is contained, conduct a post-mortem review.

What went wrong?

What worked?

What can be improved?

Use these lessons to strengthen your defences and refine your plans.

Each breach is a chance to become stronger and smarter.

Cyber resilience isn't about avoiding every attack—it's about bouncing back.

It's about knowing that no matter what happens, you have the tools, the team, and the plan to recover.

Resilience turns fear into confidence and setbacks into opportunities for growth.

Cybercriminals count on disarray.

They exploit panic and unpreparedness to amplify their impact.

Resilience takes that power away.

It puts you in control, even in the face of the unexpected.

For family offices, resilience isn't just a strategy—it's a necessity.

It's how you protect your wealth, your reputation, and your legacy.

Prepare for the worst, and you'll always be ready for the best.

Chapter 15 - Emerging Technologies in Cybersecurity.

Cybercriminals are evolving.

Cybercriminals are faster, smarter, and more sophisticated than ever.

To stay ahead, wealthy families and family offices need more than just firewalls.

Emerging technologies like artificial intelligence, biometrics, and blockchain are redefining how we fight cyber threats.

These tools are not just the future of cybersecurity—they are the present, and they are powerful.

Artificial intelligence is transforming cyber defence.

Traditional systems rely on set rules, but cybercriminals know how to exploit them.

AI changes the game by learning, adapting, and acting in real time.

AI-powered tools scan networks constantly, spotting patterns and anomalies that humans might miss.

They can detect a hacker's subtle movements, flag suspicious behaviour, and even predict attacks before they happen.

For family offices, AI provides an unmatched layer of vigilance, working 24/7 without fatigue or oversight.

Biometrics adds another level of security by making access personal.

Passwords can be stolen, but your fingerprint, face, or voice is unique.

Biometric systems verify identity with incredible accuracy, whether it's unlocking devices, authorising transactions, or securing sensitive areas.

Cybercriminals can't replicate your fingerprint or voice with the same precision, making biometrics a powerful defence.

For family offices, using biometrics means ensuring that only authorised people can access critical systems, documents, or funds.

Blockchain technology, often linked to cryptocurrencies, is a rising star in cybersecurity.

At its core, blockchain creates a secure, unchangeable ledger of data.

Transactions are recorded across multiple systems, making it nearly impossible for cybercriminals to alter or delete information.

For family offices, blockchain can protect sensitive records, track transactions, and ensure data integrity.

It also prevents fraud by providing a clear, tamper-proof history of activity.

These technologies don't work in isolation.

When combined, they create a multi-layered defence that's stronger than any single tool.

AI can monitor biometric systems for unusual activity, ensuring they aren't bypassed.

Blockchain can enhance AI by verifying data authenticity, giving algorithms a trustworthy foundation to work from.

Together, these technologies amplify each other, creating a cyber defence that's both proactive and resilient.

Adopting these tools requires more than investment—it requires strategy.

Start by identifying where your current defences fall short.

Are you vulnerable to insider threats?

Do you struggle to detect attacks in real time?

Match the technology to the problem, and integrate it into your existing systems.

Emerging tools work best when they complement, not replace, traditional defences.

Training remains critical.

Advanced technology is only as effective as the people using it.

Ensure your team understands how to interact with these tools, interpret their alerts, and respond appropriately.

AI might detect a threat, but it's up to your team to act on that information.

Biometrics can secure access, but your staff must know how to use it without creating bottlenecks.

Blockchain secures records, but your team needs to handle and store keys securely.

No technology is infallible, but emerging tools shift the balance of power.

Cybercriminals rely on speed and surprise.

AI reduces their window of opportunity by detecting threats instantly.

Biometrics denies them access to systems, even with stolen credentials.

Blockchain removes their ability to manipulate data, making their attacks less effective.

Cybercriminals are also using advanced tools, including AI, to improve their attacks.

This arms race makes adopting cutting-edge technology even more important.

The same AI that detects threats can predict and counter attacks powered by AI.

The same biometrics that secures systems can also thwart cybercriminals trying to mimic authorised users.

Blockchain, designed for transparency and security, can expose fraudulent activity faster than traditional systems.

Emerging technologies are not just a defence—they're an advantage.

They make your family office harder to target and force cybercriminals to move on to easier prey.

The cost of these tools is an investment in safety, reputation, and peace of mind.

In today's world, where threats evolve faster than ever, staying still is not an option.

Cybersecurity has moved beyond firewalls.

AI, biometrics, and blockchain are your next lines of defence. They are the tools that turn the tide in your favour.

They are the difference between reacting to a threat and staying ahead of it.

The future of cybersecurity is here, and it's time to use it to your advantage.

The question isn't whether you can afford these technologies.

It's whether you can afford to be without them.

Chapter 16 - The Role of Third-Party Advisors

No family office operates in a vacuum.

Cybersecurity is complex, and managing it alone is risky.

Cybercriminals are constantly evolving, using sophisticated tools and tactics to breach even the most secure systems.

To stay ahead, you need experts on your side.

Third-party advisors—cybersecurity specialists, managed services providers, and auditors—offer the expertise and vigilance needed to protect your wealth, reputation, and legacy.

Cybersecurity experts bring specialised knowledge to the table.

They understand the latest threats, tools, and techniques better than anyone else.

Their job is to stay ahead of cybercriminals, identifying risks and creating defences tailored to your family office.

These advisors can evaluate your current systems, spot weaknesses, and recommend improvements.

They don't just install software; they design strategies that fit your unique needs.

Managed services providers take day-to-day security off your plate.

They monitor your systems, detect threats, and respond quickly to attacks.

Their 24/7 oversight ensures nothing slips through the cracks.

Managed services offer a proactive approach, catching issues before they become problems.

For family offices, this means peace of mind, knowing your systems are always being watched by professionals.

Cybersecurity auditors play a crucial role in evaluating your defences.

They review your policies, procedures, and systems to ensure they meet the highest standards.

Auditors identify gaps in your security and help you close them.

Their insights can uncover risks you didn't know existed.

Regular audits also show stakeholders—family members, staff, and partners—that you take cybersecurity seriously.

Choosing the right advisors requires careful evaluation.

Not all experts are created equal, and not all managed services providers or auditors will fit your needs.

Look for advisors with a proven track record, relevant certifications, and experience working with family offices.

Ask for references and case studies to see how they've handled challenges similar to yours.

Trust is essential, but so is verification.

A good advisor doesn't just provide services—they become a partner.

They work closely with your team to understand your goals and priorities.

They communicate clearly, avoiding technical jargon that confuses rather than clarifies.

They provide actionable recommendations and explain why each step matters.

This collaboration ensures that everyone is aligned and focused on protecting what matters most.

Integrating third-party advisors into your operations requires trust and transparency.

Share your goals, concerns, and expectations upfront.

Give them the access they need to do their job effectively.

At the same time, set clear boundaries and define roles.

Regular check-ins keep the partnership on track and ensure you're getting the value you expect.

Cybersecurity is not a one-time fix—it's an ongoing process.

Threats evolve, and so must your defences.

Third-party advisors stay ahead of these changes, updating your systems, training your staff, and refining your strategies.

Their expertise ensures you're not just reacting to threats but actively preventing them.

Working with advisors also gives you an external perspective.

It's easy to miss risks when you're immersed in daily operations. An outsider can see blind spots and challenge assumptions.

They bring fresh ideas and solutions to the table, helping you stay ahead of emerging threats.

Their independence also provides an extra layer of accountability, ensuring your defences are as strong as possible.

Cybercriminals often target family offices because they know resources are limited compared to large corporations.

Third-party advisors level the playing field.

They give you access to the same tools, knowledge, and defences that big companies use.

Their expertise allows you to punch above your weight, making your family office a much harder target.

Regular reviews with your advisors ensure your cybersecurity remains effective.

Technology changes quickly, and what works today might not work tomorrow.

Schedule quarterly or annual check-ins to discuss updates, review performance, and plan for future needs.

Use these sessions to address new challenges, from insider threats to advancements in hacking techniques.

Third-party advisors are not just a safety net—they are an investment in resilience.

Their expertise protects your systems, reduces risks, and ensures continuity even in the face of a breach.

They allow you to focus on what matters most—managing wealth, building legacy, and maintaining trust—while they handle the complexities of cybersecurity.

Cybercriminals thrive on gaps and oversights.

Third-party advisors close those gaps, offering the specialised skills and constant vigilance your family office needs.

By partnering with the right experts, you take control of your security, stay ahead of threats, and safeguard the future.

Cybersecurity isn't just a technical issue—it's a business imperative.

With the right advisors, it's also an advantage.

Action Plan:

1. **Adopt Emerging Technologies:**
   - Use AI-driven tools for threat detection.
   - Explore biometric authentication and blockchain for data security.

2. **Engage Experts:**
   - Partner with third-party advisors for audits, monitoring, and incident response.
   - Include managed services providers to handle day-to-day security.

3. **Enhance Monitoring:**
   - Set up 24/7 monitoring for unusual activity across all systems.
   - Use tools to detect and respond to threats in real-time.

4. **Plan for Resilience:**
   - Regularly test your business continuity and incident response plans.
   - Ensure backups are secure, encrypted, and regularly tested.

Checklist:

- [ ] Deploy AI-powered monitoring tools.
- [ ] Evaluate biometric authentication and blockchain applications.
- [ ] Partner with a trusted third-party cybersecurity provider.
- [ ] Test and update your response and recovery plans regularly.

Section 5

The Bigger Picture

Chapter 17 - Regulations and Compliance.

Cybersecurity is no longer just about protecting your systems—it's about following the rules.

Governments and regulators around the world have introduced strict privacy laws and data protection standards.

These rules are designed to safeguard personal information, but they also carry serious penalties for non-compliance.

For family offices managing wealth and sensitive data, understanding these regulations isn't optional—it's essential.

Privacy laws like the GDPR in Europe, the CCPA in California and the Australian Privacy Regulation set the standard for how personal data should be collected, stored, and shared.

These laws require organisations to handle information responsibly and transparently.

They give individuals more control over their data, including the right to access, correct, or delete it.

Ignoring these rights can lead to fines, lawsuits, and damaged trust.

Data breaches carry more than just financial risks.

Regulators expect organisations to report breaches quickly and accurately.

Failing to notify authorities or affected individuals in time can result in penalties that hurt both your finances and your reputation.

It's not enough to fix the problem—you must also show that you acted responsibly throughout the process.

Compliance requires knowing what data you have, where it's stored, and how it's used.

Family offices handle a wealth of sensitive information, from personal details to financial records.

Start by conducting a data audit.

Identify every piece of data your office collects, how it's stored, and who has access.

This audit is the foundation of your compliance efforts, helping you understand your risks and responsibilities.

Access control is key to meeting compliance standards.

Limit who can view or edit sensitive information.

Use role-based access to ensure that only authorised people handle critical data.

This reduces the risk of accidental exposure and demonstrates that you've taken steps to protect privacy.

Encryption is another essential tool.

Regulations often require that sensitive data be encrypted, both in transit and at rest.

Encryption ensures that even if data is intercepted or stolen, it remains unreadable without the proper key.

It's a straightforward way to show regulators that you're serious about safeguarding information.

Regular training helps your team understand compliance requirements and their role in meeting them.

Many breaches result from human error, like clicking on a phishing link or mishandling sensitive files.

Educate your staff on best practices for data protection, including how to recognise threats and follow secure procedures.

Well-trained employees are your first line of defence and a critical part of your compliance strategy.

Vendor relationships also play a role.

If your family office works with third-party providers, their compliance practices affect you.

Regulators may hold you responsible for breaches caused by your vendors.

Before partnering with any external service, ensure they meet the same standards you follow.

Include compliance terms in your contracts and verify that they're adhering to them.

This step protects your office from unnecessary risks.

Compliance doesn't end with meeting current regulations.

Laws evolve, and what's acceptable today might not be tomorrow.

Stay informed about changes in privacy laws and standards, especially in the regions where you operate.

Appoint someone in your organisation to monitor updates and ensure you remain compliant.

This proactive approach saves you from scrambling to catch up when new rules take effect.

Reporting and documentation are critical for proving compliance.

Regulators expect clear records showing how you protect data and respond to incidents.

Keep logs of access controls, security measures, and breach response activities.

These records not only help you stay organised—they also demonstrate your commitment to accountability.

Audits are your chance to test and improve your compliance efforts.

Conduct regular internal audits to identify weaknesses and fix them before regulators or cybercriminals find them.

External audits by independent experts provide an unbiased view of your practices and help you stay on track.

Treat audits as opportunities, not threats—they're a chance to strengthen your systems and build trust with stakeholders.

Compliance isn't just about avoiding penalties.

It's about protecting the people whose data you handle.

Clients, family members, and partners trust you to keep their information safe.

Meeting regulatory standards shows that you take this responsibility seriously.

It builds confidence and sets you apart as a leader in security and transparency.

Non-compliance carries heavy costs.

Fines for violating GDPR can reach up to €20 million or 4% of global turnover, whichever is higher.

The reputational damage from a compliance failure can be even worse, especially for a family office where trust is everything.

By following the rules, you avoid these risks and reinforce your commitment to excellence.

Regulations may seem burdensome, but they exist for a reason.

They push organisations to adopt better practices, protect privacy, and prepare for evolving threats.

For family offices, compliance is not a box to tick—it's an opportunity to demonstrate leadership in a world where cybersecurity matters more than ever.

Meeting compliance standards doesn't just protect you from penalties—it protects your reputation, your relationships, and your legacy.

By following the rules and embracing a culture of responsibility, you turn a legal requirement into a strategic advantage.

Compliance isn't a challenge—it's a commitment to doing things right. And that's a standard worth upholding.

Chapter 18 - Philanthropy, ESG, and Cybersecurity

Cybersecurity isn't just about protecting your assets—it's about protecting your values.

For family offices engaged in philanthropy or pursuing environmental, social, and governance (ESG) goals, strong digital practices are a must.

Cybercriminals don't just target wealth; they target reputations and the causes you support.

A breach can do more than cost money—it can derail your mission and damage the trust you've built.

Philanthropy thrives on trust. Donors, partners, and communities depend on your ability to safeguard their information and your plans.

A cyberattack that leaks donor records or disrupts a project's funding can do lasting harm.

Cybercriminals know this, and they exploit it.

Protecting your digital systems ensures your work continues uninterrupted and your relationships remain strong.

ESG principles focus on sustainability, responsibility, and governance.

Cybersecurity aligns with these goals by fostering ethical practices and ensuring long-term resilience.

A secure digital foundation supports transparency, protects stakeholder interests, and upholds your commitment to doing business the right way.

In today's interconnected world, ignoring cybersecurity risks undermines ESG efforts.

Cybercriminals often target philanthropic organisations and ESG initiatives because they assume these groups are less secure.

Family offices managing these efforts must prove them wrong.

A breach not only exposes sensitive data but can cast doubt on your ability to manage resources effectively.

Strong cybersecurity demonstrates that you take these responsibilities seriously.

Digital sustainability matters too.

Outdated systems consume more energy and are less efficient.

Investing in modern, secure technologies reduces your environmental footprint while enhancing your defences.

Cloud-based solutions, for example, offer scalability and efficiency, minimising waste while improving security.

Aligning your cybersecurity strategy with sustainable practices reflects your values and sets an example for others.

The social aspect of ESG is built on accountability and trust.

Protecting personal data and ensuring ethical use of information shows respect for the people you serve.

Cybersecurity isn't just a technical issue—it's a human one.

When you secure your systems, you're safeguarding the individuals and communities who depend on you.

This commitment strengthens your social impact and reinforces your role as a responsible leader.

Governance is where cybersecurity and ESG intersect most directly.

Good governance means managing risks, protecting assets, and maintaining transparency.

Cybersecurity is a cornerstone of this effort.

Clear policies, regular audits, and proactive measures show that you're serious about managing digital risks.

Stakeholders notice, and they value organisations that prioritise governance in every area.

Philanthropic projects often involve partnerships, and every partner is a potential link in your security chain.

Vet your collaborators carefully, ensuring they meet your cybersecurity standards.

Include clear agreements about data protection and incident response.

A breach at one partner can ripple through the entire network, so shared responsibility is critical.

Donors expect accountability, and a secure digital infrastructure provides it.

Use encryption to protect donor data, limit access to sensitive information, and monitor systems for unusual activity.

These steps show donors that their contributions are safe and their trust is well-placed.

Strong cybersecurity can even encourage larger commitments by demonstrating your professionalism and foresight.

In ESG reporting, cybersecurity highlights your commitment to resilience and ethical practices.

Share how your family office protects data, supports sustainable technology, and upholds stakeholder trust.

These actions align with ESG goals and add depth to your reporting, showing that you take a holistic approach to governance and impact.

Cybercriminals see philanthropic and ESG-focused organisations as easy targets, but they don't have to be.

By prioritising cybersecurity, you make your office a harder target and protect the causes that matter most.

Every secure system, every encrypted file, and every trained staff member contributes to a safer, stronger organisation.

Cybersecurity and ESG aren't separate efforts—they reinforce each other.

Both require long-term thinking, ethical practices, and a commitment to doing things right.

By integrating cybersecurity into your philanthropic and ESG strategies, you protect not just your digital assets but your values, your vision, and your legacy.

In a world where reputations can be damaged with a single breach, strong cybersecurity is a non-negotiable part of leading responsibly.

It's how you protect what you've built, support what you believe in, and inspire trust in those who look to you for leadership. Secure your systems, and you secure your impact.

Chapter 19 - Cybersecurity in a Borderless World

In today's borderless world, wealth and business don't stay confined to one country. International investments, global travel, and cross-border operations create endless opportunities, but they also bring risks.

Cybercriminals thrive on complexity, and the global nature of your activities gives them more ways to strike.

Cybersecurity is no longer local—it's global, and it must evolve to keep pace.

Every country has different cybersecurity laws and standards.

What's secure in one nation might not meet the requirements of another.

Managing international operations means navigating these differences while maintaining a unified defence.

Ignoring local laws can lead to fines, delays, or breaches.

Staying compliant isn't just about avoiding penalties—it's about ensuring your systems are as secure as possible, wherever they operate.

When you travel, your risk increases.

Public Wi-Fi at airports, hotels, and cafes is a favourite target for cybercriminals.

These networks are often unsecure, making it easy for attackers to intercept your data.

Always use a virtual private network (VPN) when connecting to public Wi-Fi.

A VPN encrypts your data, keeping it safe from prying eyes.

Travel with devices that are secure, updated, and stripped of unnecessary data.

If a device is lost or stolen, your sensitive information shouldn't go with it.

Cross-border investments bring another layer of complexity.

Transactions often involve multiple parties, systems, and jurisdictions.

Each one adds a potential weak point.

Cybercriminals target these transactions, knowing that the involvement of multiple stakeholders can create delays and confusion.

Protecting international deals means using encrypted communications, secure file-sharing platforms, and robust identity verification processes.

A single breach can derail a deal and damage your reputation.

Working with international vendors and partners introduces risk as well.

Every vendor has its own cybersecurity practices—or lack of them.

A breach at one vendor can spread across the supply chain.

Before partnering with anyone, evaluate their security measures.

Require clear agreements that outline how they will protect your data and respond to incidents.

Trust is important, but verification is essential.

Different time zones can also complicate incident response.

If a breach happens while your primary team is asleep, valuable time can be lost.

Build a response plan that accounts for global operations.

Identify local contacts who can act quickly and keep communication channels open at all hours.

Speed matters in cybersecurity, and a global response team ensures you're ready no matter when or where an attack occurs.

Currency and language differences can also play into cybercriminals' hands.

Fake invoices or phishing emails in foreign currencies or languages can be harder to spot.

Train your staff to recognise these tactics and verify all financial transactions, especially those involving international accounts.

A quick phone call or email to confirm authenticity can save millions.

International regulations are another challenge.

Laws like Europe's GDPR or Australia's Privacy Act set strict standards for handling data.

Failing to meet these standards can lead to heavy fines and damaged reputations.

Ensure your cybersecurity practices align with the laws of every country you operate in.

Appoint someone to monitor changes in international regulations and keep your systems compliant.

Cybersecurity isn't static, and staying informed protects your global operations.

Cybercriminals often operate across borders, making it difficult to track or prosecute them.

International cooperation among law enforcement agencies is growing, but it's still limited.

This means prevention is your best defence. Invest in tools that detect and stop threats before they spread.

Firewalls, endpoint protection, and advanced monitoring systems are essential for managing risks in a borderless world.

Your data flows across borders too.

Cloud storage, email servers, and online platforms often operate in multiple countries.

Know where your data is stored and ensure those locations comply with your security standards.

Use encryption to protect data as it moves and consider local data centres for sensitive information to reduce exposure.

Staff training is critical for managing global risks.

Teach employees how to stay secure when traveling, handling cross-border transactions, or working with international partners.

Awareness is your strongest defence, and a well-trained team can stop breaches before they start.

Make cybersecurity a priority at every level, from frontline staff to the boardroom.

A global mindset is essential for effective cybersecurity.

Cybercriminals don't respect borders, and your defences must be just as fluid.

Protecting your family office in a borderless world means staying vigilant, adaptable, and proactive.

The risks are real, but with the right approach, they are manageable.

Cybersecurity in a global context is challenging, but it's also an opportunity.

By building strong, scalable defences, you protect your assets, your reputation, and your ability to operate anywhere in the world.

Cybercriminals may see opportunity in a borderless world, but so do you.

Stay one step ahead, and the world becomes your advantage, not your vulnerability.

Action Plan:

1. **Ensure Compliance:**
   - Understand and meet local and international data protection laws.
   - Regularly review your compliance with regulations like GDPR or Australia's Privacy Act.

2. **Integrate Cybersecurity into ESG Goals:**
   - Show how secure practices align with governance and social responsibility.
   - Use sustainable technology to reduce environmental impact.

3. **Protect Global Operations:**
   - Secure data during international travel with VPNs and encrypted devices.
   - Vet global vendors for strong security practices.

4. **Communicate the Importance:**
   - Share your cybersecurity efforts in ESG and philanthropic reporting.
   - Highlight the steps you're taking to safeguard operations and data.

Checklist:

- [ ] Conduct a compliance audit and address any gaps.
- [ ] Include cybersecurity measures in ESG strategy and reporting.
- [ ] Train staff to manage international risks during travel or cross-border operations.
- [ ] Evaluate and improve vendor cybersecurity across global partnerships.

Section 6

Securing the Future

Chapter 20 - The Cyber-Safe Family Office of Tomorrow

Protecting your family's legacy means more than growing wealth.

It means safeguarding the systems, trust, and reputation that make everything possible.

In a world where cyber threats are constant, the family office of tomorrow must be resilient, adaptive, and secure.

Building this future requires more than just tools—it demands a mindset that puts cybersecurity at the centre of everything you do.

Start by understanding that cybersecurity is not a one-time fix. It's an ongoing commitment.

Cybercriminals evolve, and so must your defences.

Regular audits, updated tools, and continuous training ensure you stay ahead of threats.

A family office that embraces change doesn't just survive—it thrives.

Prioritise simplicity in your systems.

Complex processes often create vulnerabilities.

Streamline your workflows, reduce unnecessary access, and eliminate outdated software.

A lean system is easier to protect and harder for cybercriminals to exploit.

Simplicity doesn't mean sacrificing capability—it means building smarter, stronger defences.

Trust is the foundation of every family office.

Cybersecurity strengthens that trust. When family members, staff, and partners know their data and systems are secure, confidence grows.

Transparency about your efforts reinforces this trust.

Share how you protect assets, respond to threats, and plan for the future.

This openness shows you take your responsibilities seriously.

Focus on building a culture of awareness.

The people in your family office are your greatest strength—and your biggest vulnerability.

Teach them how to spot phishing emails, use strong passwords, and recognise risks.

Make cybersecurity part of their routine, not an occasional chore.

A vigilant team is a powerful defence against even the most sophisticated attacks.

Invest in technology that adapts as threats change.

Tools like artificial intelligence, encryption, and advanced monitoring systems offer protection that grows with your needs.

These tools are not just expenses—they are investments in the longevity of your operations.

Use them wisely, and they will repay you many times over.

Prepare for the unexpected.

No system is invincible, and breaches can happen.

Have a clear response plan that covers containment, communication, and recovery.

Test this plan regularly to ensure it works when you need it most.

A prepared office bounces back quickly, turning potential disasters into minor setbacks.

Think long-term.

Cybersecurity isn't just about today's threats—it's about securing the future.

Plan for how technology will evolve and how your family office will adapt.

Stay informed about emerging risks and invest in systems that can handle tomorrow's challenges.

The future belongs to those who are ready for it.

Don't let fear drive your decisions.

Cyber threats are serious, but they are manageable.

With the right strategies, you can turn risks into opportunities to strengthen your operations.

Confidence comes from knowing you've done everything possible to protect your legacy.

The cyber-safe family office of tomorrow isn't built on luck—it's built on action.

Every step you take today, from training staff to updating systems, is a step toward securing the future.

Cybercriminals thrive on inaction.

By staying proactive, you ensure that your family's wealth, reputation, and legacy remain intact for generations to come.

Legacy is more than money—it's trust, impact, and the values you pass on.

Protecting that legacy means embracing cybersecurity not as a burden but as a responsibility.

The actions you take today will shape the story of your family tomorrow.

Make it a story worth telling.

And Finally - Securing What Matters Most

Cybersecurity is no longer just a technical issue—it's a defining responsibility for wealthy families and the offices that support them.

The stakes are personal, and the risks are real.

A single breach can compromise wealth, tarnish reputations, and erode trust built over generations.

But the good news is this, with knowledge, preparation, and the right strategies, these threats can be managed, mitigated, and even prevented.

This book has taken you through the landscape of cybercrime, the vulnerabilities that wealthy families face, and the solutions needed to protect what you value most.

From understanding the threats to building robust defences, creating awareness, and embracing advanced technologies, you now have the tools to act decisively.

Cybersecurity is not about fear—it's about empowerment.

It's about ensuring that your family's wealth, reputation, and legacy remain secure in an increasingly digital world.

The challenges of cybersecurity will continue to evolve, but so will the opportunities to strengthen your defences.

Staying vigilant, proactive, and informed is key to staying ahead.

A secure family office doesn't just protect against attacks; it builds confidence, fosters trust, and sets a standard for others to follow.

As you move forward, remember that cybersecurity is not a one-time effort but an ongoing journey.

The actions you take today will shape the future for generations to come.

Your legacy deserves the highest level of protection, and the steps you take now will ensure it remains intact and thriving.

This is your call to action. Cybersecurity is within your control, and the responsibility is yours to carry.

Embrace it fully, and you'll not only safeguard your wealth but also inspire trust, demonstrate leadership, and secure what matters most.

Let your family office be a beacon of resilience and excellence in a world that demands nothing less.

The future is yours to protect—start today.

Contents

Preface 3
Chapter 1 - The Modern Digital Battlefield 8
Chapter 2 - The Anatomy of Cybercrime... 12
Chapter 3 - Why Wealthy Families Are High-Value Targets 16
Chapter 4 - Lessons from Real Cyber Attacks..................................... 20
    Action Plan: 24
    Checklist: 24
Chapter 5 - Identifying Vulnerabilities 26
Chapter 6 - Protecting Non-Financial Assets 31
Chapter 7 - Inside-Out Risks, ... 36
Chapter 8 - The Ripple Effect! 41
    Action Plan: 45
    Checklist: 45
Chapter 9 - Cyber Hygiene 101. 47
Chapter 10 - Cybersecurity, A Tailored Approach 51
Chapter 11 - Building Your Cyber Toolkit! 56
Chapter 12 - Creating a Culture of Cyber Awareness 61
    Action Plan: 65
    Checklist: 65
Chapter 13 - Staying One Step Ahead! 67
Chapter 14 - Cyber Resilience. 71
Chapter 15 - Emerging Technologies in Cybersecurity....................... 75
Chapter 16 - The Role of Third-Party Advisors 79
    Action Plan: 83
    Checklist: 83

Chapter 17 - Regulations and Compliance. 85
Chapter 18 - Philanthropy, ESG, and Cybersecurity 90
Chapter 19 - Cybersecurity in a Borderless World 94
    Action Plan: 98
    Checklist: 98
Chapter 20 - The Cyber-Safe Family Office of Tomorrow 100
And Finally - Securing What Matters Most 103

www.ingramcontent.com/pod-product-compliance
Lightning Source LLC
Chambersburg PA
CBHW050321230526
45471CB00005B/2285